UFGS 08 56 46.10 20: Radio Frequency Shielded Enclosures, Demountable Type

Department of Defense: United States of America

The BiblioGov Project is an effort to expand awareness of the public documents and records of the U.S. Government via print publications. In broadening the public understanding of government and its work, an enlightened democracy can grow and prosper. Ranging from historic Congressional Bills to the most recent Budget of the United States Government, the BiblioGov Project spans a wealth of government information. These works are now made available through an environmentally friendly, print-on-demand basis, using only what is necessary to meet the required demands of an interested public. We invite you to learn of the records of the U.S. Government, heightening the knowledge and debate that can lead from such publications.

Included are the following Collections:

Budget of The United States Government
Presidential Documents
United States Code
Education Reports from ERIC
GAO Reports
History of Bills
House Rules and Manual
Public and Private Laws

Code of Federal Regulations
Congressional Documents
Economic Indicators
Federal Register
Government Manuals
House Journal
Privacy act Issuances
Statutes at Large

```
**************************************************************************
USACE / NAVFAC / AFCESA / NASA          UFGS-08 56 46.10 20 (August 2011)
                                        --------------------------------
Preparing Activity:  NAVFAC             Superseding
                                        UFGS-08 56 46.10 20 (April 2006)
```

UNIFIED FACILITIES GUIDE SPECIFICATIONS

References are in agreement with UMRL dated October 2012
```
**************************************************************************
```

SECTION TABLE OF CONTENTS

DIVISION 08 - OPENINGS

SECTION 08 56 46.10 20

RADIO FREQUENCY SHIELDED ENCLOSURES, DEMOUNTABLE TYPE

08/11

-- End of Section Table of Contents --

```
*************************************************************************
USACE / NAVFAC / AFCESA / NASA          UFGS-08 56 46.10 20 (August 2011)
                                        --------------------------------
Preparing Activity:  NAVFAC             Superseding
                                        UFGS-08 56 46.10 20 (April 2006)
```

UNIFIED FACILITIES GUIDE SPECIFICATIONS

References are in agreement with UMRL dated October 2012
```
*************************************************************************
```

SECTION 08 56 46.10 20

RADIO FREQUENCY SHIELDED ENCLOSURES, DEMOUNTABLE TYPE
08/11

```
*************************************************************************
```
NOTE: This guide specification covers the
requirements for radio frequency shielded
enclosures, demountable Type.

Adhere to UFC 1-300-02 Unified Facilities Guide
Specifications (UFGS) Format Standard when editing
this guide specification or preparing new project
specification sections. Edit this guide
specification for project specific requirements by
adding, deleting, or revising text. For bracketed
items, choose applicable items(s) or insert
appropriate information.

Remove information and requirements not required in
respective project, whether or not brackets are
present.

Comments, suggestions and recommended changes for
this guide specification are welcome and should be
submitted as a Criteria Change Request (CCR).
```
*************************************************************************
```

```
*************************************************************************
```
NOTE: This guide specification covers the
requirements for radio frequency shielded
enclosures, demountable Type, in sizes under 50
square meter 500 square feet. For larger enclosures
and for High Altitude Electromagnetic Pulse (HEMP)
protected enclosures, contact NAVFAC Engineering
Innovation and Criteria Office (Code EICO) before
beginning design. Do not design HEMP enclosures
utilizing demountable shield construction. The
electrical designer should refer to MIL-HDBK-419
Volumes I and II for special grounding and bonding
requirements for EMI enclosures and to NACSIM 5203
for TEMPEST enclosures. All metallic electrical
conduits which penetrate a TEMPEST shield must be
isolated within 50 mm 2 inches of the exterior of
the shield by a nonmetallic conduit section at least
150 mm 6 inches long to prevent conduction of
information from the shielded enclosure. Although

not addressed in this specification, it is
recognized that fiber optic cable has gained
acceptance as an effective method of transmitting
data across the boundary of shielded enclosures
without filtering. If fiber optic cable is used,
describe the penetration of the shield in detail.
For a discussion of the advantages and disadvantages
of fiber optic systems see NAVFAC DM-12.02.
Designer should consult these documents and other
appropriate sources before applying this guide
specification to large scale EMI enclosures to HEMP
and to TEMPEST Projects. The potential requirement
for thermal expansion joints inherent to large scale
enclosures is not addressed in this guide
specification. The extent and location of the work
to be accomplished and wiring, equipment, and
accessories necessary for a complete installation
should be indicated on the project drawings.
****

****
NOTE: The following information shall be shown on
the project drawings:

1. Assembly details;

2. Penetration details;

3. Location and method of mounting shielded
enclosure within building;

4. Location of mechanical and electrical equipment
within shielded enclosure;

5. Interior wall finish;

6. Suspended ceiling; and

7. Raised computer floor.
****

PART 1   GENERAL

1.1   REFERENCES

****
NOTE: This paragraph is used to list the
publications cited in the text of the guide
specification. The publications are referred to in
the text by basic designation only and listed in
this paragraph by organization, designation, date,
and title.

Use the Reference Wizard's Check Reference feature
when you add a RID outside of the Section's
Reference Article to automatically place the
reference in the Reference Article. Also use the
Reference Wizard's Check Reference feature to update
the issue dates.

The publications listed below form a part of this specification to the
extent referenced. The publications are referred to within the text by the
basic designation only.

AIR MOVEMENT AND CONTROL ASSOCIATION INTERNATIONAL (AMCA)

AMCA 210   (2007) Laboratory Methods of Testing Fans
                                  for Aerodynamic Performance Rating

ASTM INTERNATIONAL (ASTM)

ASTM A653/A653M   (2011) Standard Specification for Steel
                                  Sheet, Zinc-Coated (Galvanized) or
                                  Zinc-Iron Alloy-Coated (Galvannealed) by
                                  the Hot-Dip Process

ASTM B194   (2008) Standard Specification for
                                  Copper-Beryllium Alloy Plate, Sheet,
                                  Strip, and Rolled Bar

ASTM E84   (2012a) Standard Test Method for Surface
                                  Burning Characteristics of Building
                                  Materials

ASTM E90   (2009) Standard Test Method for Laboratory
                                  Measurement of Airborne Sound Transmission
                                  Loss of Building Partitions and Elements

ASTM F1066   (2004e1; R 2010) Standard Specification
                                  for Vinyl Composition Floor Tile

INSTITUTE OF ELECTRICAL AND ELECTRONICS ENGINEERS (IEEE)

IEEE 299   (2006) Standard Method for Measuring the
                                  Effectiveness of Electromagnetic Shielding
                                  Enclosures

NATIONAL FIRE PROTECTION ASSOCIATION (NFPA)

NFPA 70   (2011; Errata 2 2012) National Electrical
                                  Code

U.S. DEPARTMENT OF COMMERCE (DOC)

DOC/NIST PS51   (1971) Hardwood and Decorative Plywood

DOC/NIST PS58   (1973) Basic Hardboard (ANSI A135.4)

U.S. DEPARTMENT OF DEFENSE (DOD)

MIL-PRF-15733   (2010; Rev J, Supp 1 2010) Filters and
                                  Capacitors, Radio Frequency Interference,

General Specification for

MIL-STD-220   (2009; Rev C) Method of Insertion Loss
                     Measurement

MIL-STD-461   (2007; Rev F) Requirements for the Control
                     of Electromagnetic Interference
                     Characteristics of Subsystems and Equipment

1.2   GENERAL REQUIREMENTS

```
****************************************************************************
            NOTE:  Insert additional details describing the
            specific project for which this specification is
            being used.  Projects involving military
            communications equipment must be designed to
            incorporate the applicable requirements of
            MIL-STD-188-124, "Grounding, Bonding and Shielding
            for Common Long Haul/Tactical Communication
            Systems."  Be aware that standard manufactured
            shielded doors are not designed for exposure to
            weather.
****************************************************************************
```

Section 26 00 00.00 20 BASIC ELECTRICAL MATERIALS AND METHODS, applies to
this section, with the additions and modifications specified herein. The
enclosure[s] shall be capable of being erected, disassembled, and reerected
entirely from its interior without special tools [, except where RF
enclosure ceiling is specified as being supported by the structural ceiling
above]. Provide enclosure[s] complete with [power line filters,]
[telephone/signal line filters,] [RF air vents,] [penetrations for
compressed air lines, water lines and [_____],] [coaxial cables,] [lighting
fixtures,] [workbenches with convenience outlets,] and door assembly.
Provide each item with fittings and hardware necessary for a complete and
operable RF shielded enclosure. Where two or more units of the same type,
class, and size of equipment are required, these units shall be products of
a single manufacturer. Provide means of completely isolating the structure
electrically from the building in which it is to be installed.

1.2.1   Mechanical Work

```
****************************************************************************
            NOTE:  Modify or delete these paragraphs as required
            for each project.  Additional items such as raised
            computer floors may be specified in the same manner.
****************************************************************************
```

```
****************************************************************************
            NOTE:  Insert appropriate Section number and title
            in blank below using format per UFC 1-300-02,
            "Unified Facilities Guide Specifications (UFGS)
            Format Standard".
****************************************************************************
```

Provide complete shielded enclosure[s] including work specified in [_____]
[and [_____]].

1.2.2 Electrical Work

Conform to the requirements of the NFPA 70, National Electrical Code.
Provide a complete shielded enclosure[s] including work specified in
[_____] [and [_____]].

1.2.3 Acoustical Ceiling System

Provide as specified in Section 09 51 00 ACOUSTICAL CEILINGS.

1.3 SUBMITTALS

****

Government approval is required for submittals with a "G" designation;
submittals not having a "G" designation are [for Contractor Quality Control
approval.][for information only. When used, a designation following the
"G" designation identifies the office that will review the submittal for
the Government.] The following shall be submitted in accordance with
Section 01 33 00 SUBMITTAL PROCEDURES:

SD-02 Shop Drawings

   Radio frequency shielded enclosure

      Include penetration details.

SD-03 Product Data

   Telephone and signal line filters

   Shielded air vents

   Lighting fixtures

   Exhaust fan

   Door assemblies

SD-06 Test Reports

****
         NOTE: When specifying nonlatching doors, delete
         door static load and sag tests and cycle test for
         door latches. Retain cycle test for door hinges.
****

   Door static load test

   Door sag test

   Swinging door closure test

   EMI tests for line filters

      Submit final report to Resident Officer in Charge of
   Construction within 30 days following completion.

   Attenuation testing

   Seam leak detection testing

      The results of EMI testing shall be submitted to the Contracting
   Officer on a daily basis and test results incorporated into a EMI
   Shielding Test Final Report. Submit final reports within 30 days
   following completion of tests. List location of the permanent
   SELDS test leads.

SD-07 Certificates

Performance test plan

Qualifications of installation supervision personnel

Qualifications of testing agency

Certification of test equipment

Components of shielded enclosure individually and as a system, meet specified attenuation requirements.

SD-10 Operation and Maintenance Data

Shielded enclosure, Data Package 3[; G][; G, [_____]]

Submit in accordance with Section 01 78 23 OPERATION AND MAINTENANCE DATA.

1.4   RELIABILITY

Reliability to maintain high shielding effectiveness for long term usage with minimum maintenance shall be stressed throughout the design, construction, and erection of the specified shielded enclosure. Particular attention shall be paid to the total project so that corrosion and the installation of electrical service, power line filters, ventilation, and connector panels do not derate the required shielding effectiveness. The enclosures will be subject to varying moveable live floor loads and continuous use of the ventilation system and ac power line filters.

1.5   DELIVERY AND STORAGE

Deliver materials to the job site in undamaged condition. Store material to ensure proper alignment, and protect material against dampness and accumulated moisture before and after delivery. Store materials under cover in a well-ventilated enclosure, and do not allow materials to be exposed to extreme changes in temperature and humidity. Do not store materials in the building until concrete and masonry are dry.

1.6   QUALITY ASSURANCE

1.6.1   Certificates

1.6.1.1   Performance Test Plan

Submit a performance test plan for SELDS and IEEE 299 testing of the facility. The test plan shall include tester qualifications, equipment listings (including calibration dates and antenna factors), and proposed test report format. The plan shall also address specific dates and durations that testing will be conducted during the overall construction period so that the expert Government witness may be scheduled to observe the testing and so that repairs may be made to the shield and retests conducted before the building finish materials are installed. Finally, the test plan shall indicate the proposed dates and duration of the lowest and the highest frequency tests following installation of the building finish materials [so that an expert Government witness may be available for these final acceptance tests].

1.6.1.2   Qualifications of Testing Agency

Submit the experience and qualifications of an independent testing agency
for review and approval. The testing agency shall have recent experience
in Shielded Enclosure Leak Detection System (SELDS) and IEEE 299 shielded
enclosure testing and shall list where and when the experience was
obtained. Submit with the performance test plan.

1.6.1.3   Certification of Test Equipment

Certify that test equipment for the attenuation testing has been calibrated
within last 12 months.

1.7   MAINTENANCE

1.7.1   Contents

In addition, the manual shall contain the following information:

a.   A complete set of assembly and disassembly drawings;

b.   A schedule of recommended maintenance and adjustment procedures to
     ensure continuous shielding effectiveness;

c.   Allowable loads on top of room and on shelves mounted on walls,
     including permissible weights of equipment that can be mounted on
     walls; and

d.   Prescribed method of handling panels, cleaning of seams and contact
     fingers, bonding jumpers, installing metallic items penetrating the
     shielding material without decreasing the attenuation characteristics.

PART 2   PRODUCTS

2.1   SHIELDED ENCLOSURE CHARACTERISTICS

2.1.1   Radio Frequency Interference Attenuation

The attenuation and shielding effectiveness requirements apply to the
finished shielded enclosure[s] and enclosure's components when all power
line filters are installed and carrying current, ventilation systems are
operating, [the coaxial connector panels capped,] and shielded door[s] are
in normal operation position. The specified shielded effectiveness shall
be achieved without using conductive tapes, gaskets, or cement materials.
Provide enclosure[s] having the following minimum magnetic, electric, and
plane wave attenuation:

Magnetic - [60] [_____] dB at 14kHz increasing linearly to [100] [_____] dB
     at 200 kHz

Electric - [100] [_____] dB from 1.0 kHz to 50 MHz

Plane Wave - [100] [_____] dB between 50 MHz and 10 GHz

2.1.2   Sound Transmission Class (STC)

****
              NOTE: STC 30 provides only minimum sound
           transmission loss. For greater sound control, more

                    detailed acoustical design requirements must be
                    incorporated into the specification.
****
Provide enclosure[s] having an STC of [30] [_____] dB minimum when tested
according to ASTM E90 [not including sound transmission loss of surrounding
building construction].

2.2   PANELS CONSTRUCTION

Flat steel sheet laminated to each side of a 20 mm 3/4 inch structural core
of either plywood or hardboard. [Panels shall have a flame spread rating
of less than 25 when tested according to ASTM E84.]

2.2.1   Flat Steel Sheet

ASTM A653/A653M with Z180 G-60 coating, minimum 24 gage, phosphatized.

2.2.2   Plywood

DOC/NIST PS51 for exterior, sound grade hardwood, Type I.

2.2.3   Hardboard

DOC/NIST PS58 for standard type hardboard.

2.2.4   Adhesive for Laminating Steel Sheets to Structural Core

Waterproof type which maintains a permanent bond for the lifetime of the
enclosure.

2.2.5   Floor Finish

****
            NOTE: Indicate or specify whether other flooring is
            to be provided or higher floor loads are required.
            This is most critical when raised floors are
            required. Allowances must be made for elevated door
            thresholds. Vinyl composition 1 is asbestos-free
            and should be specified for all projects.
****

Vinyl-composition tile, ASTM F1066, Type IV, composition 1, 300 by 300 mm,
3 mm 12 by 12 inches, 1/8 inch, thick.

2.3   FRAMING-JOINING SYSTEM

The panels shall be joined and supported by specially designed members that
clamp the edges of the panels and provide continuous, uniform, and constant
pressure contact against the shielding elements of the panels. The walls
shall be self-supporting from floor to ceiling with no bracing. Deflection
of walls under a static load of 35 kg 75 pounds applied normal to the wall
surface at any point along the framing members shall not exceed 1/250 of
the span between supports. [Ceilings shall be self-supporting from wall to
wall.] [Ceilings shall be supported by adjustable, nonconducting, isolated
hangers from the structural ceiling above.] Ceilings shall be designed to
have a deflection under total weight, including ceiling finish, of not more
than 1/270 of the span. At corner intersections of walls, floor, or
ceiling, provide a one-piece factory prewelded corner section or trihedral

corner framed with brass machined cast corner cap assemblies consisting of inner and outer parts. The modular enclosure shall be designed for ease of erection, disassembly, and re-assembly.

2.3.1   Channels

The framing-joining system members shall consist of 3 mm 1/8 inch zinc-plated steel channels having minimum 16 mm 5/8 inch overlap along each side of the contacting surface. Screw fasteners shall be spaced at 75 or 100 mm 3 or 4 inch intervals.

2.3.2   Screw Fasteners

Screw fasteners shall be either zinc-plated or cadmium-plated steel, minimum size 6 mm 1/4 inch - 20 with pan or flat Phillips heads. Fasteners shall be heat treated and hardened with minimum tensile strength of 930 MPa 135,000 psi.

2.4   DOOR ASSEMBLIES

****
           NOTE: Do not accept doors that deviate from this
           specification without consulting NAVFAC 15C.
           Probable deviations include: magnetic and
           electromagnetic doors, other non-finger stock type
           doors, adhesive mounted finger stock, and requests
           to approve doors tested to less than 10,000 open
           close cycles, among others.
****

The enclosure door shall be nonsagging and nonwarping and shall afford shielded effectiveness equal to the rest of the enclosure when the door is closed. The shielded door shall be provided with [multiple rows] [at least one row] of RF finger stock around the door or its frame. The fingers that form a contact between the door and its frame shall be protected from damage due to physical contact and shall be concealed within the door and frame assemblies. The door shall have a clear opening of [900 mm] [36 inches] [_____] wide and [2100 mm] [84 inch] [_____] high. Door assembly shall be the same manufacture as the enclosure. Doors shall be reinforced steel or laminated type. Laminated type shall be the same construction as enclosure panels, except the steel faces shall be electrically and mechanically joined by channels or overlapping seams, both of which shall be continuously seam welded along all joined surfaces.

2.4.1   Finger Stock

Contacts for doors shall be copper beryllium conforming to ASTM B194, Condition HT. The finger stock shall be secured to the door or frame without using special tools or soldering or adhesives and shall have a minimum overlap of 50 mm 2 inches.

2.4.2   [Latching Type

****
           NOTE: Select the applicable paragraph(s) from the
           following:
****

****

The door shall be lever controlled with roller cam action requiring not
more than 90 N 20 pounds of operating force on the handle for both opening
and closing. The door shall be equipped with a two or three-point latching
mechanism that provides proper compressive force for the RF seal. The
mechanism shall be operable from both sides of the door and shall have
permanently-lubricated ball bearings at points of pivot and rotation. The
door latches and hinges shall be rated for a minimum of 10,000 cycles
without loss of attenuation and without adjustments.]

[Nonlatching Type

The door shall be equipped with three heavy-duty ball bearing hinges and a
door pull. Door shall open and close with a force not to exceed 20 N 5
pounds.]

2.5   LINE FILTERS

2.5.1   Power Line Filters

Shall conform to the requirements of Section 26 35 46.00 20 RADIO FREQUENCY
INTERFERENCE POWER LINE FILTERS and shall have current and voltage ratings
as [indicated] [specified].

2.5.2   Telephone and Signal Line Filters

MIL-PRF-15733. Filters shall have an insertion loss of 100 decibels in the
frequency range of 14 kHz to 10 GHz measured according to MIL-STD-220, full
load condition. Filters shall have a pass band of [_____] kHz to [_____]
kHz with a characteristic impedance of [_____] ohms.

2.6   WAVEGUIDE-TYPE AIR VENTS

Honeycomb-type air vents shall have cores fabricated of brass or steel, and
each guide shall be electrically and mechanically bonded to all adjacent
guides. Air vents shall be a permanent part of the shielded enclosure and
shall have a shielding effectiveness equal to that of the total enclosure.
Static pressure drop through the vents shall not exceed 5 Pa 0.02 inch
water gage at an air velocity of 3 m/s 600 feet per minute.

2.7   GROUNDING STUD

Enclosure shall have a permanently installed, solid brass or bronze
grounding stud complete with hardware and jamb nuts located in the entrance
plate [unless otherwise specified or indicated]. The stud shall be 13 mm
1/2 inch diameter double-threaded bolt which allows a full 50 mm 2 inch

running thread inside and outside of the shielded enclosure.

2.8 SERVICE ENTRANCE PLATES (SET-UP PANELS)

Shall be minimum 3 mm 1/8 inch thick steel, sized [300 by 300 mm] [12 by 12 inches] [_____] and shall have a 6 mm 1/4 inch extruded brass frame for mounting to shielded enclosure wall panel.

2.9 NAMEPLATES

Major components of equipment shall have manufacturer's name, address, catalog number, model, style, and type on a plate securely and conspicuously attached to each item of equipment. Nameplates for electrical apparatus shall conform to NEMA Standards.

2.10 LIGHTING

****
          **NOTE: In shielded enclosures where electronic
          equipment is very sensitive to EMI, specify a dual
          lighting system so that fluorescent lighting can be
          turned off and incandescent lighting left on during
          sensitive tests or operations.**
****

Provide lighting fixtures as indicated [and as specified in Section 26 51 00 INTERIOR LIGHTING]. Fluorescent lighting fixtures shall meet the requirements of MIL-STD-461, Class C3, Group I for both conducted and radiated interference.

2.11 EXHAUST FAN

****
          **NOTE: This paragraph cites only minimum
          requirements. Design calculations are necessary to
          size HVAC to suit room size and equipment/personnel
          contained within. Exhaust fan motors located inside
          shielded enclosure must meet MIL-STD-461, Class C3,
          Group I.**
****

Propeller fans shall be [direct drive] [belt drive] for [wall or window] [roof or ceiling] mounting, except that fans shall be centrifugal type with aluminum housing and wheel. Additionally exhaust fans shall be electromagnetically compatible. Motors shall be completely shielded from the air stream. Provide exhaust opening and gravity closing type automatic louvers. Provide exhaust which can supply 15 room air changes per hour. Capacity of fans shall be certified in accordance with AMCA 210, and shall be not greater than 110 percent of the indicated capacity at indicated pressure drop.

2.12 COAXIAL CABLE PENETRATIONS

For each coaxial cable entering the shielded enclosure, provide RF waveguide threaded insert with cap and chain on shielded room side of enclosure.

2.13   SOURCE QUALITY CONTROL

2.13.1   Door Static Load Test

The door shall be mounted and latched to its frame, then set down in a
horizontal position such that the door will open downward and only the
frame is rigidly and continuously supported from the bottom. A load of 2kPa
40 psf shall be applied uniformly over the entire surface of the door for
at least 10 minutes. The door will not be considered acceptable if this
load causes breakage, failure, or permanent deformation which varies the
clearance between door leaf and stops to vary more than 2 mm 1/16 inch from
the original dimension.

2.13.2   Door Sag Test

The door and its frame shall be installed normally and opened 90 degrees.
Two 23 kg 50 pound weights, one on each side of the door, shall be
suspended from the door within 125 mm 5 inches of the outer edge for at
least 10 minutes. The door will not be considered acceptable if this test
causes breakage, failure, or permanent deformation which varies the
clearance between the door leaf and floor frame more than 2 mm 1/16 inch
from its original dimension.

2.13.3   Swinging Door Closure Test

Door shall be operated 5000 complete open-close cycles. The door will not
be acceptable if the closure test causes any breakage, failure, or
permanent deformation that causes the clearance between door and frame to
vary more than 2 mm 1/16 inch from the original dimension.

PART 3   EXECUTION

3.1   INSTALLATION

3.1.1   Installation Supervision

Furnish the services of a qualified installation engineer or technician
regularly employed by the shielding manufacturer/fabricator for a minimum
of three 8 hours working days to instruct Contractor personnel in the
installation of the RFI shield. A qualified installation technician is
acceptable in lieu of a qualified installation engineer. After the
shielded enclosure has been completely installed including RF filters,
vents, and exhaust fans, furnish the services of the engineer or technician
described herein to inspect the installation for compliance with the
specifications. The inspection shall be made before any finishes or the
concrete topping coat are installed.

3.1.2   Panel Installation

Lay panels in a straight line with true, level, and even surfaces and with
the joints in alignment; install them in accordance with the shielding
manufacturer's recommendations. Exercise care while handling and
installing metal shielding panels to ensure that panels are not damaged.

Clean exposed surfaces of all dirt, finger marks, and foreign matter
resulting from manufacturing processes, handling, or installation. Inside
the enclosure, mount items including boxes, conduits, fixtures, and
switches directly to the RF panels with 16 mm 5/8 inch long, zinc-plated,
self-tapping screws. Keep electrical conduits as close to RF shielding as
possible. Do not use framing-joining system bolts to mount material and
equipment. If material and equipment penetrate shielded enclosure, seam
weld or solder materials and equipment to both shielding surfaces.

3.1.3   Surface Preparation

Clean and buff surfaces to ensure good electrical contact with shielding
surface. Remove paint or other coverings on mating surfaces of special
boxes such as for fire alarm systems, buzzers, and signal lights, including
areas between box and cover, box and wall, and box and conduit. Remove
insulating material to maintain a low-resistance ground system and to
ensure firm mating of metal surfaces.

3.1.4   Floor Panel Setting

Place a polyethylene film of 6-mil thickness over the structural floor of
the parent room before any other work is set thereon. Provide a 3 mm 1/8
inch thick layer of hardboard over this film with joints loosely butted.
Over this layer provide an additional layer of similar filler material of
equal thickness as the projection of the framing-joining member from the
bottom surface of the floor panel leaving no more than 6 mm 1/4 inch space
between the hardboard and the framing-joining member.

3.2   FRAMING-JOINING SYSTEM

Tighten screws with a calibrated adjustable torque wrench so that equal
torque can be set on each screw. (Proper torque values will be
approximately 9 Nm 80 inch pounds, but may vary somewhat depending on the
manufacturer).

3.3   DOOR ASSEMBLIES

Mount so that the clearance between the door edges and frame shall not vary
more than 2 mm 1/16 inch and the innerface of the door periphery does not
vary more than 2 mm 1/16 inch from the plane of the face of the stop.
Through-bolt hinges to the door and the frame.

3.4   LINE FILTERS

Provide filters for incoming electrical power lines [, including neutrals,]
and for incoming telephone and signal lines. Support filters independently
of the shielding.

3.5   WAVEGUIDE-TYPE AIR VENTS

[Provide each inlet and return air duct with the number and size of
waveguide-type air vents at each location where the ducts enter the
shielded enclosure.] [As a minimum, provide each enclosure with one 300 mm
 12 inch square and one 300 mm 12 inch square return waveguide-type air
vent.]

3.6   EXHAUST FAN

Mount on [wall] [or] [ceiling] over the exhaust vent on the exterior surface of shielded enclosure. Provide power from electrical source exterior to the shielded enclosure.

3.7   CONDUCTOR INSTALLATION

Provide filtered conductors in conduit, except for coaxial cables, from filter to shielding and penetrate the enclosure through threaded rigid steel conduits. [Twist conductors leading from the filters and conductors inside the shielded enclosure approximately 10 turns per foot in the conduit.]

3.8   GROUNDING

```
**************************************************************************
                NOTE:  If not specified in Division 16,
                "Electrical," the following sentence shall be added:
                "Wires inside the enclosure and for a distance of at
                least 15 meters 50 feet outside of the enclosure
                shall be enclosed in a grounded, threaded rigid
                steel conduit system."
**************************************************************************
```

Extend the grounding stud through and [bolt] [weld] it to the electrical power panel with a minimum No. 4 AWG insulated stranded copper conductor to effectively serve as a single grounding point for the completely assembled shielded enclosure, both internally and externally.

3.9   SERVICE ENTRANCE PLATE

Install RF connectors for coaxial cable and other RF shielded cable on entrance plate. Soft solder connectors to the plate. If location of plate is not indicated, mount plate in wall panel adjacent to power line filters.

3.10   FIELD TESTS

3.10.1   Seam Leak Detection Testing

```
**************************************************************************
                NOTE:  SELDS testing the seams in the floor
                shielding is usually very difficult because you
                cannot "sniff" on both sides (assuming the shield is
                on the ground level).  To circumvent this problem
                SELDS loops may be positioned beneath the floor
                shield for SELDS testing.
**************************************************************************
```

Continuously test seams during fabrication using the SELDS, commonly known as a "sniffer." Upon completion of the basic shielded enclosure, before applying any metal primer or installing any accessories, test the entire shielded enclosure with the SELDS. Install terminal points on the shielding exterior and permanently attach test leads on two sets of diagonally opposing corners during construction for use with the SELDS. Continuously probe seams with the test receiver set to detect abrupt change of shielding level greater than 10 dB on the "shielding unit" scale. Clearly mark points having change greater than 10 dB and repair the seam to meet the specified requirement. Retest each repaired point until there are no points on seams which fail test.

3.10.2   Attenuation Testing

[Furnish the services of an independent testing laboratory, approved by the Contracting Officer, to test the shielded enclosure. Certify that laboratory is equipped and staffed to perform field tests of RF shielded enclosures and performs the tests as a normal service.] [Final acceptance testing will be by the Government.] Conduct the final shielding acceptance test after penetrations have been completed, specifically including electrical and other utility penetrations. In addition, the Contractor may schedule a complete or abbreviated test to verify that the shielding assembly is adequate prior to conducting final shielding acceptance test.

3.10.2.1   Test Method

****
        NOTE: Expert Government witness should be present
        for all final acceptance testing. Note that IEEE
        299 requires one magnetic field test (150 kHz),
        three electric field tests (200 kHz, 1 MHz, 18 MHz),
        and one plane wave test (400 MHz). Also, note that
        IEEE 299 and NSA 65-6 differ on positioning of
        source and receiver. IEEE 299 requires source
        outside and receiver inside the shield, while NSA
        65-6 requires source inside and receiver outside (to
        simulate TEMPEST conditions). For TEMPEST shielding
        effectiveness testing, continuous sweeping of seams
        at one or more plane wave frequencies should also be
        specified, in addition to testing around all door
        panels, filters, air duct penetrations and all other
        penetrations of the shielding at all test
        frequencies. If enclosure is designed specifically
        for attenuating microwave frequencies, specify
        additional test frequencies above 1 GHz. Such
        testing is expensive and should only be used when a
        firm requirement exists (e.g., NSA-65-6).
****

The test procedure, frequencies, and equipment shall be as specified in IEEE 299 [plus the additional frequencies specified in the contract]. Perform the test as soon as possible after completion of the shielded enclosure, including installation of services, power/telephone/signal lines, RF filters, and waveguide vents. Conduct tests with doors closed and the filters under normal load conditions.

3.10.2.2   Additional Test Points

****
        NOTE: Use this paragraph if design includes strict
        tolerances, high attenuation requirements, and many
        penetrations.
****

Measure additional test points beyond those specified in IEEE 299. Test points include the periphery of doors and covers, handles, latches, power filter penetrations, air vent filters, telephone and control line filter penetrations, and points of penetration by pipes, tubes, and bolts.

3.10.3   Final In Service Testing

Upon completion of acceptance checks, settings, and tests, show by
demonstration in service that equipment and devices are in operating
condition and performing the intended function. Give the Contracting
Officer five working days advance notice of the dates and times for checks
and tests.

-- End of Section --

Lightning Source UK Ltd.
Milton Keynes UK
UKHW031819111019
351459UK00005B/157/P

9 781288 756438